SAO MIGUEL

AZORES

TRAVEL GUIDE 2023 2024

The Ultimate Guide For First Time Visitors To Explore The Island's Natural Beauty, History, Cuisine, Top Attractions And Other Travel Experiences

Rick M. Driver

Disclaimer

Copyright © by Rick M. Driver 2023
All rights reserved.

Table Of Contents

Map of Faial Island

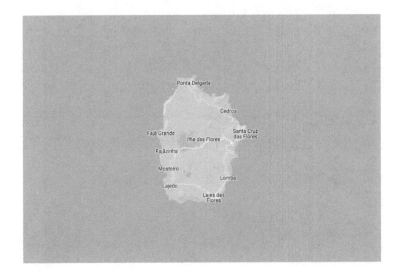

Map of Ponta Delgada

Introduction

Sao Miguel, the largest island in the Azores archipelago, is a hidden jewel, a place of untamed beauty, and undiscovered wonders, located in the center of the wide Atlantic Ocean. Imagine a place with rolling hills of lush greenery, turquoise lakes surrounded by volcanic craters, and falling waterfalls that produce a symphony of the gentle sounds of nature. This is more than simply a place to go; it's a magical tapestry of encounters just waiting to be weaved into your tale.

A calmness overtakes you as soon as you arrive at Sao Miguel's shoreline. The healing environment of the island immediately lifts your burden of the outside world. An escape like this has several advantages. Hiking the trails of Sete Cidades, where the Blue and Green Lakes reflect the colors of the sky, can be a life-changing experience for those with a sense of adventure. Walking among the island's varied flora and animals deepens one's connection to nature and oneself.

However, Sao Miguel is not just for adventure seekers. Natural hot springs on the island, a gift from the island's volcanic core, provide rest and renewal. With its brilliant botanical wonders, the renowned Terra Nostra Gardens offer a serene haven for reflection and rejuvenation.

However, it goes beyond the beauty of the island's landscape. Azorean hospitality and its rich cultural past weave an exquisite tapestry that beckons you to join it. Every experience is a stroke on the canvas of your memories, whether it is enjoying a traditional cozido das furnas, a meal cooked by the earth's geothermal heat, or taking part in regional festivals packed with music and dancing.

We reveal the island's mysteries in the Sao Miguel Azores travel guide, assisting you in creating your own account of this paradise. Sao Miguel offers all of this and more, whether you're looking for comfort in the embrace of nature, excitement in its untamed landscapes, or a chance to immerse yourself in a culture that hasn't changed much over the years. Your trip to Sao Miguel is more than simply a vacation; it's a voyage of self-discovery that will inspire you and open a new chapter in your life.

Map of Sao Miguel

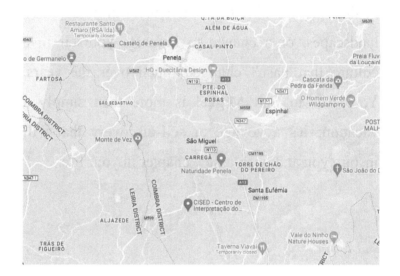

Chapter 1: Overview Of Sao Miguel

History of Sao miguel

After Prince Henry the Navigator commanded that cattle be brought ashore on seven islands in the archipelago, the first colony in Sao Miguel was established in 1444. Gonçalo Velho Cabral, a knight and friar of the Order of Christ, was given command of it. Later, North Afrikaners, Madeirans, Jews, Moors, and probably Frenchmen joined the original settlers from the Portuguese districts of Estremadura, Upper Alentejo, and Algarve.

The island's fertile soil, strategic location at the intersection of Europe, Africa, and America, and the export of wheat to the Portuguese garrisons of North African strongholds, sugar cane, the dye-producing "woad" and "archil" plants (sold to Flanders), wine, and dairy products all contributed to the island's rapid economic growth. A century later, the island's agricultural output was expanded by the introduction of sweet potatoes, maize, yams, flax, and oranges. In the latter half of the 16th and early part of the 17th centuries, the island was attacked by French, English, and Algerian corsairs. Following the loss of a French fleet outside Vila Franca do Campo that included Portuguese sailors and supported Dom Antonio Prior to Crato's claims to the Portuguese throne, Sao Miguel was taken over by Spanish forces in 1582.

After Portugal regained its independence in 1640, Sao Miguel regained its status as a commerce hub and established ties with Brazil, where it dispatched settlement parties.

The resistance to the Absolutist rule on the Island was established in 1831, during the Liberal Wars, following the deployment of Liberal troops in Nordeste on the future Duke of Terceira's command. The Army left Ponta Delgada in 1832 after establishing the Constitution and acknowledging Maria II of Portugal as their monarch. The previous economic boom resumed after the turbulent time of the Liberal Wars, the port of Ponta Delgada was constructed, and new crops including tea, pineapple, and tobacco were also introduced. Up until the present, the improvement of agricultural products and the growth of the fishing industry both contributed to economic growth.

From the end of the 18th century, the export of oranges to England provided Sao Miguel with tremendous fortune. The local entrepreneurial spirit quickly led to the introduction of new products, including tobacco, tea, flag, chicory, sugar beet, and pineapples, which ensured the region's economic survival when the blight that began in 1860 decimated the orange groves. As the years went by, a number of industries as well as an increase in fishing and livestock raising joined these crops.

The major political and administrative hub in the Azores is located on the island, which now serves as the Presidency of the Autonomous Region of the Azores.

The Etiquettes And Culture

Warmth is the way Azoreans greet one another; even on first encounters, they frequently embrace and kiss each other on both cheeks. This represents the warmth of the island and establishes the framework for sincere connections.

The use of titles like "Senhor" (Mr.) or "Senhora" (Mrs.) followed by the person's last name is a sign of deep-seated respect for seniors. This regard can also be demonstrated by giving up your seat on a bus or train to an elderly person.

While the island's slow pace of life may cause appointments and parties to start a little bit later than expected, punctuality is still respected. These circumstances call for patience and adaptability.

When entering places of worship or other traditional settings, it is respectful to dress modestly. It is advised to err on the side of conservative when unsure about what is proper to wear. Wait for the host to start the conversation when you are eating, and always be grateful for the food. It is usual to finish your food and keep your hands visible on the table.

Despite the fact that English is widely spoken, showing some effort to acquire some fundamental Portuguese words shows respect for the community. Language barriers can be crossed by saying "Bom dia" (Good morning) and "Obrigado/a" (Thank you). When invited to someone's home, giving a gift is a kind act. The invitation is appreciated when given flowers, champagne, or chocolates.

Comparatively speaking to other civilizations, Sao Miguel has smaller personal spaces. Expect closer proximity during chats since physical touch is usual. You may fully experience Azorean culture by taking part in neighborhood events. To truly appreciate the energy of the island, embrace the joy, music, and folk dances.

Landscape

Sao Miguel is a beautiful island with numerous lakes, including the famous Vista do Rei Lookout in Sete Cidades, the Green and Blue twin lakes, Lagoa do Fogo, and the Furnas Valley. Other lakes include Canario, Santiago, Éguas, and Congro Lakes in the Serra Devassa and central region. The island also boasts stunning views of the sea, with islets like Vila Islet and Mosteiros Islet. Natural hot water pools are another attraction, with stunning locations like Caldeira Velha, Terra Nostra Park's lake, and

Caldeiras of Ribeira Grande. The Furnas Valley is a popular destination for spas and hot springs, making it a hub for spas and bottling.

Geography

The largest island in the Azores archipelago, Sao Miguel, is around 910 square miles (759 km2) in size, with a length of 40 miles (65 km) and a maximum width of 10 miles (16 km). It is located at 37° 50′ North latitude and 25° 30′ West longitude.

The island of Sao Miguel is made up of two volcanic massifs that are divided by a low-lying middle ridge. Pico da Vara (Vara Peak), which is located in the eastern massif and has an elevation of 3545 feet (1,080 meters), is the highest peak. Sete Cidades (seven cities), Fogo (fire), and Furnas are enormous craters that have magnificent lakes with clean water.

Languages Spoken in Sao miguel

Portuguese is widely spoken in Sao Miguel, Azores, as the Azores are a Portuguese-speaking territory. For regular conversations, official concerns, and business dealings, Portuguese is employed.

Although Portuguese is the primary language, many individuals working in the tourism and hospitality sector as well as younger generations frequently speak English fluently. In tourist locations, hotels, restaurants, and among people who frequently deal with tourists, English is widely spoken.

It's also important to keep in mind that, especially in areas popular with foreign tourists, you can run into people who speak other languages, such as Spanish or French, to varying degrees due to the multicultural nature of many tourist locations. However, it will typically be highly beneficial to have a basic command of either Portuguese or English for efficient communication on the island.

Useful Portuguese Phrases for Travelers

- Hello - Olá - OH-LAH
- Please - Por favor - POR FA-VOR
- You're welcome - De nada - DE NA-DAH
- Yes - Sim - SIM
- No - Não - NAOUM

- I'm sorry - Desculpa / lamento - DES-KOOL-PAH
- I don't understand - Não comprendo - NAOUM COM-PRE-EN-DOH
- How much is...? - Quanto custa...? - KWAN-TOH KOS-TAH
- Where is...? - Onde é...? - ONDE EH EH
- When? - Quando? - KWAN-DOH
- May I please have...? - Pode dar me..., por favor? - PODE DAR ME POR FAVOR
- Beer - Cerveja - SER-VE-JAH
- Wine - Vinho - VINO
- Water - Agua - AH-GWA
- Train station - Estação de comboio - ES-TA-SA DJECOM-BOY-O
- Airport - Aeroporto - AH-EH-ROH-POR-TOH
- Entrance - Entrada - EN-TRA-DA
- Exit - Saida - SIGN-DA
- Help! - Socorro! - SO-KOR-HO

- I need a doctor - Eu preciso de um médico - EU PRE-SI-ZO DE UM MEH-DE-KO
- I don't feel well - Não me sinto bem - NÃO ME SINTO BEM
- Fire! - Fogo! - FO-GO
- My name is [Your Name] - MAY-OO NOH-MEE EH [Your Name].
- Nice to meet you - Prazer em conhecê-lo - PRA-ZEHR AIN KON-YAY-SAY-LO.
- How are you? - Como está? - KOH-MOO EHS-TAH?
- Do you speak English? - Você fala inglês? - VOH-SEH FAH-LAH EEN-GLEICH?
- Can you help me? - Pode me ajudar? - POH-DEE MAY AH-ZHOO-DAR?
- A coffee, please - Um café, por favor. - OOHM KAH-FEH, POHR FAH-VOHR.
- The menu, please -O cardápio, por favor - OH KAHR-DAP-YOO, POHR FAH-VOHR.

- How much does it cost? - Quanto custa? - KWAN-TO KOO-STAH?

- Where is the bus/taxi station? - Onde é a estação de ônibus/táxi? - JOHN-DEH EH AH ES-TEH-DOWN DEH OH-NEE-BOOS/TAHK-SEE?

- I need to go to [place] - Preciso ir para [lugar] - PREH-SEE-SOH EER PAH-RAH [place].

- I'm lost - Estou perdido/a - EHS-TOH PEHR-DEE-DOO/DAH

- How much is this? - Quanto é isso? - KWAN-TOH EH EE-SOH?

- Do you accept credit cards? - Aceita cartão de crédito? - AH-SOH-TAH KAR-TÃO DEH KREH-DEE-TOH?

- Where can I find a restroom? - Onde posso encontrar um banheiro? - JOHN-DEH POH-SOH EHN-KOHN-TRAHR ROOM BAHN-YEH-ROH?

- Is it far/near? - Está longe/perto? - EHS-UTAH LONG-EH/PEHR-TOH?

- What's your name? - Qual é o seu nome? - KUAL EH OH SEU NOH-MEH?

- Can I take a photo here? - Posso tirar uma foto aqui? - POH-SOH TEE-RAHR OO-MAH FOH-TOH AH-KEE?

- Is it open/closed? - Está aberto/fechado? - EHS-TAH AH-BEHR-TOH/FEH-SHAH-DOO?

- Where is the beach? - Onde fica a praia? - OHN-DEH FEE-KAH AH PRAH-EE-AH?

- I don't know - Não sei - NOW SAY

- Can you give me a suggestion? - Pode me dar uma sugestão? - POH-DEH MAY DAHR OO-MAH SOO-ZHEHS-TAO?

- How long does it take to get there? - Quanto tempo leva para chegar lá? - KWAN-TOH TEHM-POOH LEH-VAH PAH-RAH SHEH-GAHR LAH?

- It's hot/cold today - Está calor/frio hoje - EHS-TAH KAH-LOHR/FREE-OH OH-JEE.

- I'm hungry/thirsty - Eu estou com fome/sede - AY-OO EHS-TOH KOHM FOH-MEH/SEH-DEH

- I'm tired - Estou cansado/a - EHS-TOH KAHN-SAH-DOO/DAH

- The weather is good/bad - O tempo está bom/mau - OH THEM-POOH EHS-UTAH BOHM/MAOW

- Can you help me find [place]? - Pode me ajudar a encontrar [place]? - POH-DEH MAY AH-ZHOO-DAR AH EHN-KOHN-TRAHR [place]?

- Do you recommend this restaurant? - Você recomenda este restaurante? - VOH-SEH REH-KOH-MEN-DAH EH-STEH RES-TOH-RAHN-TEH?

- It's raining/windy - Está a chover/ventar - EHS-TAH AH SHOH-VEHR/VEHN-TAHR.

The Currency Used in Sao Miguel

The Euro (€) is the unit of currency in Sao Miguel, Azores. The Azores, a self-governing territory of Portugal, use the same currency as the rest of the country. All transactions, including those for meals, lodging, and other everyday costs, are conducted in euros. Despite the fact that most businesses take credit and debit cards, it is advised to have some Euros on hand for cash transactions. ATMs are also easily accessible for cash withdrawals and currency exchange.

Chapter 2: Getting Started

When to visit Sao Miguel

The main factors to think about before visiting the Azores islands are what you want to accomplish and your budget. Many people from the mainland come to the islands throughout the summer to see family or take in the stunning surroundings. It is the busiest and most expensive season as a result of this and international tourism.

Aim for the shoulder seasons if you want a more laid-back and affordable experience because winter can have difficult weather. Keep in mind that because they are situated in the center of the ocean, the islands are particularly vulnerable to the winter storms that develop in the Atlantic, which frequently have an impact on crossings (and your plans!).

In either case, be ready to experience all four seasons in a single day whenever you go. It's possible to have a sunny and warm morning only to trek up a mountain and experience colder temps, rain, and sometimes even no visibility. Your backpack's raincoat could end up being your best friend.

Temperatures normally range from approximately 68°F to 79°F in the summer, from about 60°F to 71°F in the mid-seasons, and from about 53°F to 64°F in the winter. But be aware that particular temperatures can change depending on the island and the time of day.

Climate and Weather

The maritime setting in the North Atlantic Ocean has an impact on the climate and weather in Sao Miguel, Azores. The island experiences a temperate maritime environment with frequent weather fluctuations, high humidity, and generally mild temperatures. Here is a general description of Sao Miguel's climate:

1. Mild temperatures

Throughout the year, Sao Miguel has generally temperate temperatures. In the lower months, the average temperature is roughly 14°C (57°F), whereas in the warmer months, it is closer to 23°C (73°F).

2. Moderate Seasons

Because of Sao Miguel's oceanic impact, the traditional four seasons don't really exist there. There are still some differences, though:

- **Winter (December - February) :** Winters are moderate, with lows of 10°C (50°F) occurring infrequently. During this time, it rains a fair amount.
- **Spring (March–May) :** Spring is characterized by increased sunshine, softer temperatures, blooming flowers, and lush surroundings.

- **Summer (June to August) :** Summers are comfortable, with temperatures averaging 20 to 25 °C (68 to 77 °F). Due to the warm weather, this is the busiest travel season.
- **Autumn (September to November):** Temperatures gradually decrease in the fall, ranging from 18 to 23 °C (64 to 73 °F). Rainfall resumes increasing.

3. Humidity and Rainfall

The island's marine setting causes rather high humidity levels all through the year. Rainfall is common, particularly in the fall and winter. Particularly in places with higher elevations, fog and mist are frequent.

4. Unpredictable weather changes

The erratic weather fluctuations in Sao Miguel's climate are one of its distinctive features. One frequently encounters a variety of weather conditions in a single day, ranging from sunshine to rain and back again. Because of the island's diverse microclimates, the weather can fluctuate greatly depending on where you are.

5. Hurricanes and tropical storms

Sao Miguel may experience tropical storms or hurricanes, although this is uncommon. This is especially true from June to November, when the Atlantic hurricane season is at its peak. Severe effects are uncommon since the Azores are often well-prepared for such disasters.

Restaurants and, Bars and Cafés

The largest and most populous island in the archipelago of the Azores, Sao Miguel, has a thriving culinary heritage that is a reflection of its rich cultural past and breathtaking natural surroundings. For foodies and tourists wishing to experience the flavors and ambiance of the island, Sao Miguel provides a wide range of options, from little local eateries to fine dining venues, and quiet cafés to fashionable cocktail bars.

Restaurants

- Tony's Restaurant, Ponta Delgada
- A Tasca, Ponta Delgada
- Associação Agrícola, Furnas
- Cais 20, Ponta Delgada
- Quinta dos Sabores, Ponta Delgada
- Restaurante São Pedro, Ribeira Grande

Bars and Cafés

- Praia Café, Ponta Delgada
- Obrigado, Ponta Delgada
- Mercado da Graça, Ponta Delgada
- Mariserra, Ribeira Grande
- Blackout Cocktail Bar, Ponta Delgada
- Café Central, Ponta Delgada

Food and Drink in Sao Miguel

The culinary journey of the bars and restaurants on Sao Miguel is evidence of the island's dedication to upholding its traditions while embracing contemporary tastes and inspirations. Sao Miguel welcomes you to relish every taste and sip while immersing yourself in its vibrant culinary tapestry, which ranges from traditional Azorean fare to cosmopolitan fusion. Sao Miguel's eating scene offers an amazing exploration of cuisine and culture, whether you're looking for genuine experiences, beautiful views, or social connections with locals.

Here are some foods in Sao Miguel for tourists to enjoy:

- Azores Pineapple
- Bife à Regional (beef steak)
- Queijadas da Vila
- Cozido das Furnas
- Octopus Salad
- Sour cheese from Furnas
- Bolos Lêvedos
- Tuna Steak and lots of fresh fish
- Limpets (and lots of seafood)
- Local Spirits

Here some drinks in sao Miguel you can also have as a tourist to enjoy:

- Vinho Verde
- Vinho Tinto
- Liqueurs
- Tea
- Coffee
- Milkshakes
- Fruit Juices
- Poncha
- Azorean Craft Beer

Chapter 3: Preparing for the trip

Travel Insurance

It is crucial to take travel insurance into account when organizing your vacation to sao Miguel in the Azores. In the event that unanticipated circumstances interfere with your travel plans, travel insurance offers you financial security and peace of mind. If you decide to get travel insurance for your trip to sao Miguel, be sure to carefully review the terms and coverage information. The coverage limits, deductibles, and any exclusions should all be taken into account. Even though sao Miguel is a generally calm and tranquil location, having travel insurance can provide you the assurance to fully explore and enjoy your trip because you'll be ready for the unexpected.

Here are some good reasons to purchase travel insurance for your journey in sao Miguel:

1. Trip Cancellation and Interruption Coverage

Because of unforeseeable events like illness, injury, or a family emergency, you might occasionally need to cancel or shorten your vacation. If your plans change, travel insurance can compensate you for non-refundable costs like airfare and lodging.

2. Healthcare Costs

Despite the fact that San Miguel is a stunning place, it's crucial to have access to medical treatment in case of illness or accident. Medical charges, including doctor visits, hospital stays, and prescription drugs, can be covered by travel insurance, allowing you to receive the necessary care without concern for the cost.

3. Luggage Lost or Delayed

Travel insurance will reimburse you for the cost of replacing clothing and other necessities in the event that your luggage is delayed, damaged, or lost while you are traveling.

4. Emergency Evacuation

In the unlikely case of a significant medical emergency, travel insurance may pay for emergency medical transportation to a facility that can provide the necessary care.

5. Travel Delays

There are many different causes for flight delays or cancellations. If there are unforeseen delays, travel insurance will pay for any additional costs you incur for transportation, lodging, and food.

6. Personal Liability

Accidents might occur, and you might accidentally harm someone else or damage their property. Liability claims arising from personal conduct may be covered by travel insurance.

7. Pre-existing Medical Conditions

If you have a medical condition, you may be covered by some travel insurance policies because they provide coverage for such situations.

8. 24/7 Support

Numerous travel insurance companies provide 24-hour helplines for assistance in case of emergency. They can direct you in difficult circumstances and assist you in locating medical facilities and local legislation.

Budgeting

How much cash will you require to travel to the Azores? You should budget approximately €134 ($145) per day for your trip to the Azores, which is the average daily cost based on what other tourists spend there. The average cost of meals for one day for previous tourists was €45 ($49), and the average cost of local transportation was €30 ($33). A couple can stay in an Azores hotel for an average cost of €134 ($146). Therefore, the average cost of a weeklong trip to the Azores for two individuals is €1,872 ($2,037). These average travel costs were compiled from feedback from previous travelers to assist you in creating your own travel budget.

Money Saving Tips

Consult the money-saving advice listed below if you want to reduce the cost of your trip to the Azores as low as possible. They just involve making a few minor changes to your itinerary so that you have more money to spend on visiting the cantinas in Sao Miguel and sipping wine in Corvo. Let's look at this:

1. Travel during the off-peak season

According to statistics, flights to the Azores can cost up to 50% less in January than they would in June and July, when demand is at its highest. You can save a ton of money by traveling when most people aren't (i.e., between November and March) because that pattern is present in hotels and even with island trips.

2. Hold out for low-cost flights

Chances are, you chose a departure date that is not covered by low-cost airlines if you can't locate a flight to Ponta Delgada on the day you wish to go that costs less than $500 roundtrip. You'll almost certainly save money if you check directly with

Ryanair to see when they fly and then reschedule your trip accordingly.

3. Do free stuff

You know, dolphin-watching tours and vineyard visits don't have to cost a fortune. In the Azores, you may find hiking routes and beaches for free.

4. Book in advance

If you wait until the last minute, the cost of everything from hotels to flights may rise. Simply put, cheap rates don't incentivize impromptu travel. If you shop about, you may get the most affordable flights to the islands as well as the most affordable accommodations there.

5. Opt for self-catering lodging

There are several self-catering hotels available in the Azores, and buying local produce at the markets can significantly reduce your food costs.

Wifi and internet Availability

The majority of Sao Miguel's hotels, resorts, and guesthouses offer free WiFi to their visitors. The connection quality, however, may differ depending on the establishment. Here's a thorough investigation of WiFi and internet accessibility in Sao Miguel, covering everything from the energetic streets of Ponta Delgada to the serene sanctuaries tucked away in the island's interior.

Here's what to anticipate:

1. Restaurants and Cafés

A lot of eateries, cafés, and restaurants provide their patrons with free WiFi. In populated locations like Ponta Delgada, this is very typical.

2. Public Spaces

There may be free WiFi connections available in some public spaces, including parks, plazas, and town centers. These are frequently offered by regional governments.

3. Tourist Information Centers

In large cities, tourist information centers may provide free WiFi for guests, enabling you to stay connected while making plans for your activities.

4. Airports

Travelers can get free WiFi at Ponta Delgada's João Paulo II Airport. This is really helpful for keeping in touch before you leave or when you arrive.

5. SIM Cards and Data Plans

If you're looking for a more regular and dependable internet connection, think about obtaining a local SIM card from a local telecom operator together with a data package. You'll be able to use your mobile device to access the internet all throughout the island thanks to this.

6. Cafés and Coworking Spaces

On the island, there are some locations that specialize in providing WiFi and a relaxing workstation. Coworking areas, libraries, and particular cafés fall under this category.

7. Rural places

Rural and more remote places may have slower or less dependable internet service, compared to urban areas, which often have stronger internet infrastructure. When making your plans, keep this in mind.

Chapter 4: Accommodation Options

It makes sense to establish a base in Ponta Delgada for your journey. Despite having few natural features, it is quite well-linked and offers a ton of dining options and shopping to keep you occupied in the evenings.

Ribeira Grande is another choice. Budget hotels and high-end resorts have both opened up there recently, and the city is also a terrific hub for restaurants.

Furnas can be a better option for you if you want a more isolated experience and to get away from it all. To experience the island differently, think of staying in two distinct locations (North-South or East-West). You'll also cut down on your driving time.

Hotels

The largest and most populous island in the archipelago of the Azores, Sao Miguel Island is also the most developed in terms of tourism and receives the most visitors. It's crucial to emphasize that the Azores tourism development plans follow an ecological concern and do not cope with hotels and other tourist infrastructure that may harm the environment before we move on to Sao Miguel's best hotels. In fact, the government has prohibited the construction of several of those. The fundamental goal of the Azores is to preserve nature as it is; they are the first archipelago in the world to be acknowledged as a destination for sustainable tourism!

All travelers should visit the island, and with more and more flights from Europe and the US, you must do so immediately! Trust me, it will blow your mind! I hope to visit the Azores again soon so I can see more of the islands. However, I'm doing everything I can to get you going on your trip. You can find the following top hotels there:

- Furnas Boutique Hotel, Furnas
- Santa Barbara Eco-Beach Resort, Ribeira Grande
- Terra Nostra Garden Hotel, Furnas
- Azor Hotel, Ponta Delgada
- Sao Vicente Lodge, Sao Vicente Ferreira
- Grand Hotel Açores Atlântico, Ponta Delgada

- Pink House, Fajã de Baixo

Hostels

The warm, lively, and full-character hostels on Sao Miguel are a mirror of the island's spirit. These hostels offer a great chance to meet other travelers from all over the world, whether you're a solitary adventurer, a group of friends, or a frugal traveler.

The opportunity to become fully immersed in local culture is one of the most alluring benefits of living in a hostel in Sao Miguel. Hostels provide an opportunity to meet locals, indulge in communal meals, and take guided tours conducted by island fans who may reveal the island's hidden gems, far from the impersonal hallways of hotels.

Hostels in Sao Miguel offer advantages above and beyond simple cost and practicality. They provide an unrivaled chance to develop relationships with locals and other tourists, building a sense of community that enhances the entire travel experience. The communal areas serve as venues for telling stories, offering advice, and developing enduring relationships.

Here are some top hostels you can find in Sao Miguel:

- Orange Terrace Hostel, Ponta Delgada
- Out of the Blue Hostel, Ponta Delgada
- Ponta Delgada Youth Hostel, Ponta Delgada

- Hostel Vila Franca, Vila Franca do Campo
- Lagares Hostel, Lagoa
- Lombinho Guest House, Nordeste
- Quinta da Mo, Ribeira Grande
- Ninho de Manta Hostel, Ribeira Grande

Campsites

A camper's paradise may be found on the stunning Azores islands, which are located in the center of the North Atlantic. Two of the five campsites on the major Azorean island of Sao Miguel are free year-round, while the other three cost only a few euros per night for two people and a small tent.

The other three are close to the coast, with both beaches and swimming pools nearby, while two of the campsites are located in the craters of volcanoes with breathtaking views.

If you rent a car, getting around the island is simple. Since the island is so small, there are no railroads, but there is a bus service, and most campgrounds are close to a bus stop.

Here are some campsites in Sao Miguel:

- Sete Cidades Parque De Campismo
- Furnas Campsite
- Nordeste Campsite

Chapter 5:Transportation Options

The largest and most varied island in the Azores archipelago, Sao Miguel, has a wide range of transportation choices to make it easier for you to see its breathtaking landscapes, charming settlements, and distinctive cultural attractions. The transportation options on the island can be tailored to suit a variety of interests, whether you're looking for flexibility, convenience, or a dash of adventure. Here is a detailed overview of the available transportation in Sao Miguel:

Buses

The fastest, most affordable, and environmentally friendly method of transportation is probably by using bus lines that round the entire island. Three lines are run by three distinct businesses. Although the buses are somewhat ancient, trips rarely last longer than 90 minutes because the distances are so close together. They are often quite clean and not overly crowded.

The main avenue is conveniently served by buses that travel between the city's important locations. Smaller mini buses are used for in-town bus services, and the island's bigger touring buses are used for community-to-community transit. Both services are available along Avenida D. Infante Henriques and may be confusing to newcomers. The tourist office and bus stops each have schedules accessible.

Car Rentals

Renting a car is one of the greatest ways to explore the island. The island of Sao Miguel is small enough to drive around in a day, however many places require a vehicle. The Ponta Delgada Airport offers rental automobiles, and some rental agencies will even pick you up there and let you return the vehicle there. To prevent long lines at the rental agency or having to choose a less-than-ideal vehicle, make reservations for a car in advance.

Bike Rentals

For individuals who want to explore at their own pace, some municipalities on the island have bike rental services. Cycling may be a fun and environmentally beneficial method to get through low-lying areas and along the coast while taking in the sea air.

Scooter/Motorbike

Renting a scooter or motorcycle could be the perfect solution if you're looking for a more thrilling mode of transportation. You can maneuver through the roads of Sao Miguel on these two-wheeled vehicles while taking in the distinctive views of its scenery.

Water Taxis

Water taxis are a distinctive mode of transportation that are available in coastal areas and let you travel in a novel and picturesque way along Sao Miguel's coastline and to surrounding islets.

Horseback Riding

You can go on horseback riding tours in several parts of Sao Miguel and get a unique perspective of the island's environment. Your journey can be made a little more romantic by this equestrian experience.

Ferries

There are ferry services between Flores and Corvo as well as between Sao Miguel and Santa Maria, despite the fact that they are typically somewhat limited. Around the center group of islands, particularly Faial, Pico, and Sao Jorge, there is reliable service. Timetables can change unexpectedly during the low season, so be sure to plan ahead.

Taxis

In urban regions and well-known tourist destinations, taxis are easily accessible. For quick journeys, they provide a practical method of transportation, and many of the drivers are familiar with the culture and history of the area. A practical and affordable way to tour the Azores is by taxi. The majority of the drivers can speak English, and the cabs are often of high quality. Although cabs are often safe and regulated, it's a good idea to double-check the fare before leaving. The main routes are clearly defined, and gas is quite inexpensive.

Planes

The local airline SATA Air Azores, which circumnavigates the archipelago, connects each of the nine Azores islands, each of which has its own airport. Island hopping is made simple by scheduled aircraft that fly from one island to the next, pausing for 20 minutes at each location. Typically, Bombardiers with 40 or 80 seats and dual propellers are used.

Helicopters

Consider taking a helicopter trip for an amazing perspective of Sao Miguel's scenery. Along with transportation, these tours offer breathtaking aerial views that highlight the island's splendor.

Chapter 6: Activities

The Azores' largest and most populous island, sao Miguel offers the widest selection of activities. The island provides a lush, natural setting with beaches, lakes, mountains, and topography that is perfect for outdoor pursuits. Numerous activities are available, including two 18-hole golf courses of the highest caliber, tennis courts, rowing, windsurfing, hang gliding, scuba diving, surfing, climbing, and fishing. All of this is possible while enjoying a refreshing climate and a distinctive, multicolored landscape.

Streams and Lakes

Sao Miguel streams wind through ravines that are heavily forested, their clear water reflecting the banks' lush vegetation. Red gurnards, achigs, and aggressive trout and carp are all catchable. Trout that test any fisherman's expertise can be found in the streams of Praia, Alegria, Bispos, Faial da Terra, Guilherme, Machado, Caldeirões, Coelhas, Salga, Carneiros, Limos, and Grande. Perch, carp, and pike can be found in plenty in the Lagoa das Sete Cidades lake. Trout and carp thrive in Lagoa do Fogo, while the achiga live in Lagoa Rasa and So Bras. You can catch trout, perch, carp, red gurnards, and sandals in Lagoa das Furnas.

Underwater Life

Sao Miguel offers breathtaking cliffs, valleys, and craters together with warm, clear water. Divers and underwater explorers will undoubtedly be drawn to the rich and diverse flora and wildlife, where the dusky perch swims past the dolphin and the tortoise passes by the ray while endless shoals of fish pass by. One may find thousands of little paradises along the coast of Sao Miguel where they can enjoy all the sea's attractions during the day or at night.

Ponta da Galera, the coast near Feteiras, and the islets of Vile Franca and Mosteiros are all good locations for underwater research. A ship by the name of the Dori is submerged close to the harbor of Ponta Delgada at a depth that makes it accessible for tours.

Sea and Fishing

For those who love rock fishing, Sao Miguel is heaven because of its indented coast and its abundance and variety of fish. Barracuda, red bream, bluefish Braemar, conger eel, garfish, triggerfish, jack crevalle, mackerel, moray eel, and common sea bream are the principal species caught. There are many well-known fishing spots, but those at Ponta Delgada, Ponta das Freiras, Ferraria, Mosteiros, Ponta da Bretanha, Porto das Capelas, Poços de Sao Vicente, Rabo de Peixe, Ponta, and

Porto da Ribeira do Nordeste, Água Retorta, and Faial da Terra are among the most fascinating.

With the use of a boat, it is possible to fish for barracuda, oceanic bonito, bluefish bream, dolphin, amberjack, and many types of tuna within a short distance (2 to 3 km) off the shore. Undoubtedly, the enormous and aggressive swordfish, oceanic bream, Pecos, as well as various tuna and shark species, etc., offer opportunities for exciting fights to devoted sports fishermen. Here, a number of records have previously been broken. Ponta Delgada has boats with specialized equipment for this purpose, and they travel as far as the islets of Formigas.

Chapter 7 : Sightseeing

Best locations for hikes

There are several challenging hiking trails on this breathtaking island, which is a part of the Azores archipelago in the center of the Atlantic Ocean. Sao Miguel has everything, whether you prefer long, strenuous hikes or a relaxing stroll. So don't wait and continue reading!

In Sao Miguel, there are other hiking trails similar to that one. Therefore, you will eventually find yourself on one of them. Sao Miguel Island is not very large, so even if you get lost, a little hiking will point you in the direction of a road, a little church, or another route.

I have compiled all of the helpful advice I learned while hiking in Sao Miguel. Additionally, I have gathered all of the pertinent data for some of the top hikes in Sao Miguel. All of this is done to make it simpler for you to get around the island and have the fun of your life!

Here are some hiking locations in Sao Miguel:

- Salto do Prego
- Pico da Vara
- Rocha da Relva
- Rota da Água
- Quatro Fábricas Da Luz
- Trilho do Agrião
- Rocha Do Cascalho

Recommended itinerary for first time Tourists

My home island in the Azores is Sao Miguel. Planning a route is crucial because there are so many diverse scenery and activities in this area. This is the same route I take to show friends visiting Sao Miguel island.

When friends come to visit, I spend a large amount of time returning to my native island, Sao Miguel. It's my responsibility to keep them occupied with a well-balanced itinerary so they can enjoy their trip.

This 4-day road trip plan to Sao Miguel is the culmination of many years working as a local tour guide.

Day 1: Sete Cidades

We're going to spend today exploring the island's western side. For sete cidades, try to choose a day with clear skies; otherwise, all you'll see is clouds.

The schedule for the day is per the following:

- Vista do rei viewpoint
- Monte palace hotel
- Canario lake
- Boca do inferno viewpoint
- Sete cidades lake
- Ferraria

Day 2: Lagoa do Fogo and Ponta Delgada

This day includes a trip to Lagoa do fogo, one of the three major lakes in Sao Miguel, as well as a whale-watching tour from Ponta Delgada. You are welcome to view these sites in reverse.

- Whale-watching tour
- Ponta Delgada
- Pico da Barrosa (Barrosa Peak)
- Lagoa do fogo (Fogo Lake)
- Caldeira Velha

Day 3: Nordeste and Furnas

You'll visit the rustic Furnas Valley and the island's untamed eastern region on this day. Prepare to see, feel, and smell the Azorean volcanic phenomenon. It is not a terrible idea to include this day's itinerary on the day with the worst weather.

I strongly advise you to complete the 2-hour hiking trek in sanguinho- Salto do prego if you have more time nearby. It's among my top hikes in the Azores. The section is stunning and leads to a picturesque waterfall in the middle of a forest. This day is already jam-packed, so I didn't add it here!

- Lagoa das Furnas (Furnas Lake)
- Furnas
- Terra Nostra Park
- Furnas Thelma Spring
- Nordeste
- Ribeira dos Caldeirões

Day 4: Gorreana and Vila Franca

On day four, you should finish up any loose ends on the island to make sure you've seen Sao Miguel from every position and viewpoint possible.

Finally, if the weather allows, it's time for a swim in the ocean!

- ILhéu de Vila Franca (Vila Franca Islet)
- Lagoa do congro (Congro Lake)
- Gorreana Tea
- Porto Formoso
- Miradouro de Santa Iria (Santa Iria Viewpoint)

Tourism Festivals

Sao Miguel, the alluring crown jewel of the Azores archipelago, is more than just a place to visit; it's a memorable experience. And what better way to preserve the memories of this alluring island than by purchasing one of its distinctive and varied array of mementos? Sao Miguel provides a variety of treasures that perfectly encapsulate the character of this Atlantic paradise, from ancient customs to contemporary delights. It holds a number of tourism festivals all year long, giving guests the chance to become fully immersed in the island's culture, customs, and exuberant celebrations. These Sao Miguel tourism festivals are noteworthy:

- Festivals of Senhor Santo Cristo dos Milagres
- Saint John's festival
- Feast of Our Lady of Grace
- Semana do Mar (Sea Week)
- Festival Caloura
- Festival Monte Verde
- Festival das Marés
- Festival Músicas do Mundo

Souvenirs for tourists

In Sao Miguel, souvenirs not only make thoughtful presents but also provide concrete links to the island's culture and history. They enable visitors to take a bit of the captivating landscapes, vibrant culture, and genuine tastes of the Azores home with them. These distinctive products serve as treasured mementos of an unforgettable journey because they frequently demonstrate the expert craftsmanship and rich heritage of the Azorean people. To support the neighborhood and maintain the authenticity of your trip, think about choosing mementos manufactured by regional craftsmen.

Here are some lists of souvenirs you can find in Sao Miguel:

- Azorean Ceramics and Pottery
- Azorean Embroidery
- Azorean Knitwear
- Azorean Cheese
- Handmade Crafts
- Natural Cosmetics
- Seashell Art
- Local Honey and Jams
- Sea Salt and Spices
- Postcards and Prints

Chapter 8 : Exploring Some Top Neighboring Islands in Azores With Map

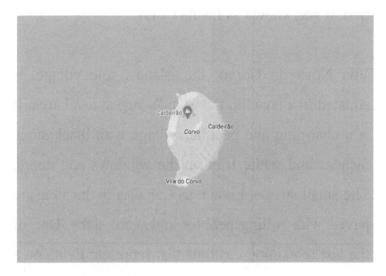

Corvo Island

Together with the island of Flores, Corvo, which is recognized by UNESCO as a World Biosphere Reserve, makes up the Western Group of the Azores archipelago. It has volcanic origins and is the smallest of the nine islands, measuring only 17.1 km2.

Around 1452, the Portuguese navigator Diogo Teive discovered Corvo and Flores simultaneously. At first, it was known as Insula Corvi.

Vila Nova do Corvo, the island's sole village, is situated in a lava faj, the island's largest level area. It is a charming and peculiar village with black stone facades and white trim on the windows and doors. The small streets, known as Canadas in the area, are paved with rolling pebbles and worn slabs. One of the last remaining customs that represent living on a tranquil island where everyone knows one another is the use of wooden locks fashioned by the craftsmen of Corvo on the doors of the homes.

It is worthwhile to visit the Corvo Visitors' Center as well as the Church of Nossa Senhora dos Milagres (the island's patron saint), which houses a painting of the Virgin and Child of Flemish origin and an ivory Indo-Portuguese crucifix.

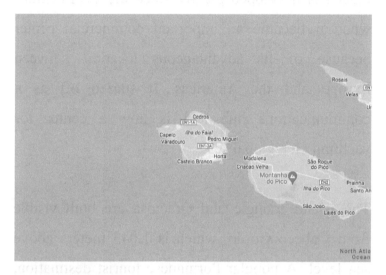

Faial Island

The "triangle islands" of So Jorge, Pico, and the gem Faial are united by the Faial Channel to form the core group of the Azores. Its area is 172 km2, and its length and width are 21 and 14 km, respectively. It was founded in 1427 and settled by Flemish people in 1432; it was given the name Blue Island and is famous for its enormous blue hydrangeas.

Faial has developed greatly since the 17th century when it became an important commercial center because of its advantageous location between Europe and the Americas. It started off as a communications hub and is now a center for yachting on a global scale.

The island triangle and Graciosa are both visible from Cabeço Gordo, which is 1,043 meters above sea level. A popular Portuguese tourist destination, the nearby Faial Natural Park is centered on the enormous Caldeira crater, which is surrounded by lush flora and blue hydrangeas. The park won an EDEN award.

Unbeatable views of Pico Island and occasionally So Jorge may be seen from Horta's strategic location. A lunar-like landscape may be seen at its westernmost point, where the massive Capelinhos Volcano, which was formed in 1957–1958, erupted. With a trip up to the lighthouse for unrivaled views, the Interpretation Center here offers a cutting-edge multimedia experience.

Horta has panoramic views of Faial's North Coast, which are impressive. The path from Praia do Almoxarife, Pedro Miguel, Ribeirinha, Cedros, Ribeira Funda, and other locations leads to a vista point with a view of Faj from the Costa Brava.

Views of Pico Island are breathtaking from Castelo Branco and Feteira, which are to the south. Horta's marina welcomes people of various cultural backgrounds, and the town itself is home to the Horta Museum, the Museum of Sacred Art, the S. Francisco, and Nossa Senhora da Carmo churches, as well as other attractions that capture the fascination of Faial.

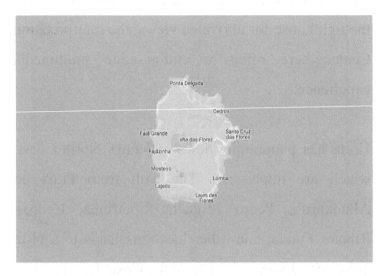

Flores Island

The westernmost region of the Azores and of Europe, Flores, is designated as a UNESCO Biosphere Reserve and offers landscapes that resemble havens. This island is a part of the western group of the Azores, together with Corvo.

The 141.4 km2 island of Flores, which is separated between the municipalities of Santa Cruz and Lajes, is a must-visit place in the Azores. It was found by Diogo de Teive sometime about 1452, and was given the name "Flores" due to the profusion of goldenrod that produced a carpet of yellow blooms all across the island.

Flores is home to several waterfalls, lakes, streams, and wells that make up a veritable treasure trove of natural treasures. The island's shoreline is rocky and severely indented.

The island is small enough to be easily traveled throughout. For a different perspective of its amazing rock formations and caves, start with a boat ride. It is excellent to view Santa Cruz das Flores Arch, the islet of Maria Vaz, Enxaréus, and Galo caverns from the water.

While scuba diving in Baixa do Amigo, Ponta da Caveira, and the islet of Garajau, divers find paradise in the Bay of Alagoa. Algares, Cabo, Mosteiros, and **Monte** Gordo rivers offer thrilling opportunities for fishing and canyoning.

Back on land, unwind at Santa Cruz's or Lajes das Flores' natural swimming holes. Choose pools like Ribeira Grande and Poço de Bacalhau, which are created at the base of waterfalls, for a more untamed experience.

Flores is a paradise for birdwatchers, especially from September to November at Lagoa Branca. Enjoy a lunch of island fare that includes items like wine, fish, island cheese, watercress soup, sausage with yams, and seafood.

Discover the seven volcanic craters in the center, which have been transformed into beautiful lakes like Lagoa Funda. Views from Morro Alto, the island's highest point, and Rocha dos Bordes, which resembles a massive pipe organ, are breathtaking.

The westernmost point of Europe is designated by the celestial navigational reference point Monchique Islet. Visit historical sites, churches, and museums in the towns of Santa Cruz das Flores and Lajes das Flores.

The Holy Spirit Feasts, Santa Cruz Celebrations, and the Lajes Emigrant Festival all provide life to the island.

Lace, embroidery, woven blankets, and hydrangea kernels from Flores provide lovely mementos that perfectly capture the spirit of the island.

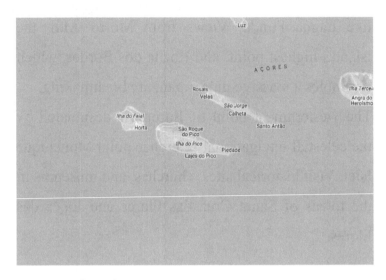

Pico Island

One of the most stunning and underappreciated islands in the Azores is Pico Island, called after its towering mountain. The "Mountain Island," which is only second in size to S. Miguel Island, dominates the Azorean central group at a distance of around 4.5 nautical miles from Faial Island and 11 miles from S. Jorge Island. It is around 167 square miles (433 km2) in size.

The traditions of Pico's whaling and winemaking have shaped the city's history. Contemporary features of Pico include the renowned Pico wines, the vineyards that have been classified as UNESCO World Heritage Sites, and the construction of wooden boats. A movement for equitable treatment research and observation of whales, dolphins, and other marine animals has replaced the long-gone practice of whaling. From Madalena or Lajes, tours for whale and dolphin watching can be arranged.

Volcanic eruptions stopped 300 years ago, and today Pico is regarded as a dormant volcano, which adds to the island's allure and attracts a lot of experts.

The beauty around this little populated island of Pico is an exquisite combination of lava rock and unique vegetation. Some of the nicest swimming holes in the Azores may be found on Pico, and a sand beach will occasionally pop up.

Pico is also the perfect island for biking and motto-quad riding, swimming, bird watching, hiking, jogging, walking, and seeing whales and dolphins. Speleology is another one of Pico's and its guests' favorite pastimes.

On Pico Island, tranquility can be found everywhere, but there is also the option of escaping to the village to take in the vibrant culture or the sporadic festival. Only one ferry ride separates trips to S. Jorge and Faial. While getting to know the smaller Faial Island takes less time, getting to know Pico takes much longer because it requires getting out of the automobile to see everything the island has to offer.

Santa Maria Island

Santa Maria and São Miguel, two islands in the Azores' Eastern Group, stand 81 kilometers apart. Santa Maria's uniqueness lies in lush fields, traditional culture, whitewashed chimneys, ochre soil, golden beaches, and azure waters.

Known as the Sunshine Island, Santa Maria's southernmost and easternmost location gifts it with a warm, dry climate, tinting vegetation yellow.

The island splits into two regions: the west, flat and home to Vila do Porto, contrasts with the rugged, vegetated east. Pico Alto, the highest point at 590 meters, offers sweeping views. This eastern area includes parishes like Espírito Santo and Santa Bárbara.

Santa Maria's geological tale is in its rocks, reflecting its being the Azores' first-formed island. Its discovery and settlement by Portuguese explorers mark its history. Fossils in Pedreira do Campo reveal its submerged past. The Dalberto Pombo Environmental Interpretation Centre showcases this. The island's "barreiros," landscapes painted in red and orange, reveal clayey beauty. Barreiro da Faneca, Raposo, Tagarete, and Cré Bays are protected areas.

Volcanic formations, like Ribeira de Maloás' waterfall, impress. Rocky headlands, steep cliffs, serene beaches like Praia Formosa, and vibrant waters define Santa Maria. Vila do Porto's historic homes feature Manueline-style doors. Nossa Senhora da Assunção Church and So Brás Fort echo history.

In Anjos, a Columbus statue and the Chapel of Nossa Senhora dos Anjos nod to American ties. Santa Maria's historic homes boast vibrant colors, shaped by Alentejo and Algarve influences. Each parish showcases distinct hues against white brickwork.

Sao Jorge Island

The neighboring islands of Pico and Faial, along with Sao Jorge, make up the "Ilhas Triangulo," or triangle-shaped group of islands in the middle of the Azores.

The long, narrow shape of Sao Jorge distinguishes it from the other Azores islands. Despite being 55 km long, it is barely 7 km wide. A tectonic plate boundary that runs 200 kilometers east to the main island of Sao Miguel and is caused by a linear volcanic fissure that gave rise to the island. The island is also known for its fajas, which are coastal plateaus where many of the smaller communities are located. In the north, where the seacliffs are the sharpest, historic landslides created the best natural swimming pools in the Azores, forming the fajas. The cliffs on the southern shore are less abrupt, and lava flows built several of the southern fajas. The best way to discover the fajas is to hike the island's superb network of hiking trails with a local guide.

When combined with neighboring Terceira, Sao Jorge is a perfect island for a split-stay. One of our most popular walking holidays is our Terceira & Sao

Jorge guided walking holiday, which lets visitors explore the stunning coastline landscapes of Sao Jorge on foot.

Chapter 9 : Exploring Some Top Neighboring Cities In Azores With Maps

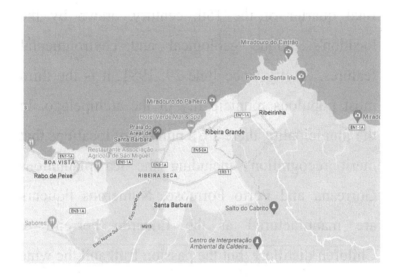

Overview Of Ribeira Grande With Tourist Map

The volcanic mountain of the Serra de Gua de Pau, whose boiler is situated in Lagoa do Fogo, dominates the relief of Ribeira Grande, which is located on the north shore of the island of Sao Miguel. Fumaroles in Caldeira Velha and the Boilers of Ribeira Grande are evidence of its volcanic origin. The first settlers arrived in the north face, which is traversed by the Ribeira Grande, in the final quarter of the 15th century, drawn by the location's unique geological and environmental features. A city since June 29, 1981, it is the third most populous municipality in the archipelago. In the municipality, there are a number of locations that merit recognition, including the tea plantations Gorreana and Porto Formoso. Numerous liqueurs are manufactured at the Eduardo Ferreira & Children distillery, but the passion fruit and the wine under the trademark "Capote's wife" stand out. The most traditional holidays in the archipelago take place from April through June. Although they vary from region to region, they always have the emperor's coronation as their starting point, the day on which gifts of bread, meat, and wine are given to the poor.

Here are some top attractions of Ribeira Grande:

- Plantacoes de Cha Gorreana
- Salto do Cabrito
- Miradouro de Santa Iría
- Caldeira Velha Environmental Interpretation Centre
- Praia de Santa Bárbara
- Tabaco da Maia Museum
- Ribeira Grande's Bridge
- Frade Viewpoint

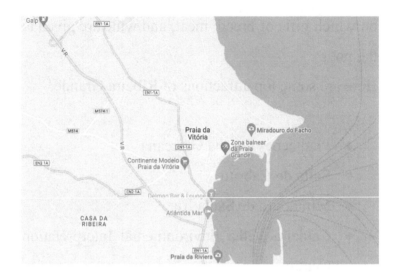

Overview Of Praia Da Vitoria With Tourist Map

The harbor city of Praia da Vitória on Terceira Island is well-known for its heritage and quaint main square. The village offers a relaxed vacation vibe, light-colored sand, and a busy marina. Early immigrants constructed the parish church, which is renowned for its Gothic entrance, Manueline style, and Baroque side chapel. The village has expansive views of the ocean and lush fields. The Furnas de

Enxofre volcanic zone, the Lajes whale Museum, and the Algar do Carvo geological reserve are all accessible to tourists. In August, the town also holds the Festas da Praia, which highlights regional culture.

Here are some top attractions of Praia da Vitória:

- Praia dos Biscoitos
- Serra do Cume Viewpoint
- Miradouro Do Facho
- Vitória Bea
- Escaleiras Beach
- Lagoa do Junco.

Overview Of Arrifes With Tourist Map

On Portugal's Sao Miguel Island in the Azores archipelago, there is a quaint settlement called Arrifes that combines natural beauty with old-world charm and a warm sense of community. The community is renowned for its breathtaking landscape, which includes hydrangea hedges and verdant green pastures. Visitors can stroll around the peaceful setting and explore the adjacent hills.

Visitors are made to feel at home in the tight-knit community, and Azorean customs are observed at local festivals. The village's churches are significant historical and architectural landmarks that demonstrate the faith and dedication of the locals. For those looking for tranquility and a connection with nature, Arrifes offers a serene refuge.

Here are some top attractions of Arrifes:

- Vista do Rei
- Lagoa do Canario
- Sete Cidates
- Pico da Cruz
- Pico das Eguas
- Boca do Inferno (Viewpoint)
- Lagoa Verde - Around the sea
- Lago Azul

Overview Of Ponta Delgada With Tourist Map

A little fishing village called Ponta Delgada was chosen as the main port for the island of San Miguel. Churches, cathedrals, and manor houses can be found in the historic district. Today, it is a global metropolis with a thriving arts and business community. The major entrance to the city is along the pricy coastal road. Ponta Delgada, an Azorean city, combines tradition, modernism, cosmopolitanism, and artifacts from more than five centuries of history.

Here are some top attractions of Ponta Delgada:

- Ponta da Ferraria
- Jardim Botânico António Borges
- Igreja do Santo Cristo
- Arruda Pineapple Plantation
- Pico Carvão
- Museu Carlos Machado museum

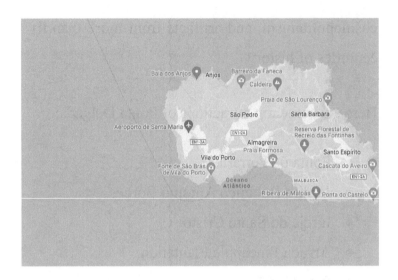

Overview Of Vila Do Porto With Tourist Map

On Portugal's Santa Maria Island is the village of Vila do Porto, which has a vibrant culture, a rich history, and stunning scenery. Its location offers breathtaking views of the Atlantic coastline and rolling hills, and its historic core is home to colorful buildings and cobblestone streets. The town's bustling harbor welcomes yachts and fishing vessels, exhibiting the maritime tradition of the island.

Additionally, Vila do Porto provides access to Santa Maria's natural wonders via walking trails and birding. Festivals and events highlight the city's vibrant culture, and tourists enjoy visiting because of how hospitable and giving the locals are.

Here are some top attractions of Vila do Porto:

- Miradouro Sao Lourenco
- Ilha a Pé
- Praia Formosa
- Farol de Gonçalo Velho
- Dalberto Pombo Environmental Interpretation Centre
- Baia dos Anjos
- Baia do Raposo

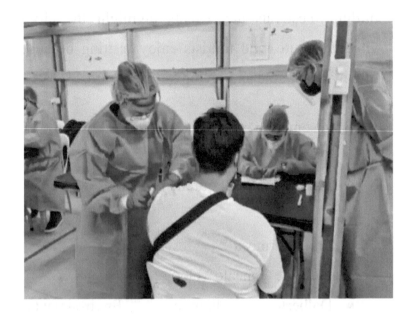

Chapter 8 : Health and Safety Precautions

Staying safe

Although there are very few reported crimes in the Azores, it is nevertheless advisable to take the typical safety precautions. The islands' inhabitants are incredibly kind, and there are few indications of poverty. Even though attacks on tourists are practically unheard of, travelers are nonetheless encouraged to keep a watch on their things, especially when in huge crowds, and to store valuables like passports and large sums of cash in hotel safes.

Both local food and tap water are safe to consume. Prior to traveling to the Azores, it is a good idea to purchase travel insurance because the islands' medical services are not all-inclusive. The hospitals in Terceira and Faial are comparable to those on the Portuguese mainland. vaccination against hepatitis is not required. If you intend to consume shellfish, which could potentially be dangerous, an injection might be helpful. Pharmacies can be found in most cities, towns, and villages, and they typically have regular hours if medication is needed.

Drug-related crimes predominate and are typically restricted to Ribeira Grande and Ponta Delgada. Though it does happen, it is wise to lock your car and keep any valuables out of sight, particularly when parking at trailheads for a long trip.

Drive with caution as many roads are narrow, have blind turns, and have steep inclines. Other dangers could be stray animals or dim lighting. Avoid dirt or poorly marked roads in unknown areas since their conditions may deteriorate at a time when it is too late to turn around and can result in catastrophic damage to your car. Pay particular attention to any warning signs regarding inclines. Some dangerous roads are frequented by thieves who want to steal from wrecked cars.

Watch out for big waves and strong undertow currents on the beaches, and heed any lifeguards or warning flags that may be posted. Unsurprisingly, the poisonous Portuguese Man 'o War has one of the greatest populations in the world in the Azores, including sao Miguel. The animals that resemble jellyfish are most prevalent in the spring, and they can be blown into protected locations by the wind. Swimmers should watch out for "floats" that resemble plastic bottles and may be tinted purple or blue. They should also be extremely cautious of anything below the ocean's surface, as these creatures' tentacles can reach distances of up to 46 m (156 feet), on average, from the float. Even if the Man 'o War is dead, its tentacles still deliver a brutal sting. Beware of tentacles buried in the sand and never approach a Portuguese Man 'o War, even if it washes up on the shore. Avoid touching the tentacles if you have been stung; instead, use ocean water to wash them off your skin. Applying cold, freshwater or urinating on the region that has been stung will only make the sting worse. Additionally, avoid using an EpiPen since this may result in a hazardous reaction. It is advised to soak the affected region in hot, Epsom salt-infused water, and to seek emergency medical assistance if a serious envenomation is noticed, such as trouble breathing, disorientation, dizziness, or acute pain.

Emergency services

In Sao Miguel, Azores, emergency services are readily available to ensure the safety and well-being of residents and visitors. If you find yourself in need of assistance, here are the primary emergency services you can contact:

Medical Emergencies

In case of a medical emergency, you can call 112, which is the general emergency number in Portugal. This number connects you to medical services, including ambulances and hospitals. The emergency services will dispatch the necessary medical assistance to your location.

Police

If you require police assistance, you can also dial 112. They will connect you to the police services for any urgent law enforcement matters.

Fire and Rescue

For firefighting and rescue services, you can dial 112. This number will connect you to the fire department, which handles fire emergencies, rescue operations, and other related situations.

It's important to note that while 112 is the universal emergency number in Portugal, including the Azores, you can also contact individual services directly using the following numbers:

- Medical Emergencies (Ambulance): 112
- Police: 112
- Fire and Rescue: 112

Additional Tips

1. When calling for emergency services, try to remain as calm as possible and provide clear and accurate information about your location and the nature of the emergency.

2. English is commonly spoken by emergency operators, but having a basic understanding of Portuguese phrases related to emergencies can be helpful.

3. If you're in a tourist area or hotel, the staff might be able to assist you in contacting emergency services as well.

4. Make sure to have your travel insurance information readily available, as this can assist you in case you need medical attention.

Immunization

When traveling to Sao Miguel, Azores, it's a good idea to make sure your immunizations are up to date to ensure your health and safety during your stay. While Sao Miguel doesn't typically require any specific vaccinations for entry, it's important to consider general vaccinations and health precautions for any international travel.

Here are some useful things to know:

Routine Vaccinations

Confirm that your routine vaccinations are updated. These may include vaccines such as measles, mumps, rubella (MMR), diphtheria, tetanus, pertussis (DTaP), varicella (chickenpox), and influenza. Check with your healthcare provider to confirm your vaccination status.

Hepatitis A and B

Hepatitis A is known as a viral disease gotten through polluted food and water. Hepatitis B is gotten through blood and other organic liquids. Depending on your travel plans and previous vaccination history, your healthcare provider might recommend these vaccinations.

Traveler's Diarrhea

Traveler's diarrhea is common when visiting new destinations. While it's not a vaccination, you can discuss with your doctor about carrying over-the-counter medications to manage this issue.

COVID-19

As of my last update in September 2021, the COVID-19 pandemic continues to impact travel. Make sure to stay updated on the current travel restrictions, testing requirements, and vaccination guidelines related to COVID-19 for your destination and departure country.

Consult Your Healthcare Provider

Before traveling to Sao Miguel, Azores, or any destination, it's recommended to consult your healthcare provider or a travel medicine specialist. They can provide personalized advice based on your health history, destination, and travel plans. They will guide you on which vaccinations are recommended and any other health precautions you should take.

Conclusion

Instead of arriving at a conclusion as we close this book, we discover ourselves on the verge of an astonishing trip. The secrets, magnificence, and soul of Sao Miguel, Azores, have been revealed by turning the pages. However, this is an invitation rather than a goodbye, a hushed promise of experiences to come.

Beyond these words, the island's scenery still beckons, its culture welcomes you with open arms, and its tales long to entwine with your own. Carry with you the essence of this guide — the direction, the wisdom, and the inspiration — as you go out to explore Sao Miguel's breathtaking natural wonders and colorful traditions.

Allow each path you take to serve as a stanza in your journey's ballad. Allow each interaction with a local to be a warm, resonant tune. Every taste of Azorean cuisine should be remembered as a story of joy.

May the chapters that make up your story of discovery, change, and enrichment in Sao Miguel be composed of the experiences you had there. May you discover that the book you finish is just a precursor to the novel you're intended to write when surrounded by the Azores' natural splendor as you immerse yourself in the wonders of the island.

Made in United States
Troutdale, OR
02/01/2024